Landforms

Volcanoes

Cassie Mayer

Heinemann Library
Chicago, Illinois

© 2007 Heinemann Library
an imprint of Capstone Global Library, LLC
Chicago, Illinois

Customer Service   800-747-4992

Visit our website at www.heinemannlibrary.com

Photo research by Tracey Engel and Tracy Cummins
Designed by Jo Hinton-Malivoire
Printed in the United States of America in Eau Claire, Wisconsin. 020615 008770R

Library of Congress Cataloging-in-Publication Data
Mayer, Cassie.
  Volcanoes / Cassie Mayer.
    p. cm. — (Landforms)
  Includes bibliographical references and index.
  ISBN-10: 1-4034-8438-4 — ISBN-10: 1-4034-8444-9 (pbk.)
  ISBN-13: 978-1-4034-8438-3 — ISBN-13: 978-1-4034-8444-4 (pbk.)
  1. Volcanoes—Juvenile literature. I. Title. II. Series.
  QE521.3.M387 2007
  551.21—dc22
                              2006004674

Acknowledgments
The author and publisher are grateful to the following for permission to reproduce copyright material:
Corbis pp. **4** (river, Pat O'Hara; mountain, Royalty Free; island, George Steinmetz; cave, Layne Kennedy), **5** (Galen Rowell), **6** (Philip Wallick), **8**, **9** (epa), **10** (Roger Ressmeyer), **11**, **12** (Larry Dale Gordon/zefa), **13** (Galen Rowell), **14** (Yann Arthus-Bertrand), **15** (Pablo Corral Vega), **16** (Yann Arthus-Bertrand), **17** (Royalty Free), **18** (Royalty Free), **19** (Jose Fuste Raga), **22** (both), **23** (crater, Galen Rowell; volcano, Larry Dale Gordon, lava, Corbis); Getty Images pp. **7** (Colin Salmon), **21** (Art Wolfe); Kraft p. **20** (Photo Researchers, Inc.).

Cover photograph of Mount Etna, Italy, reproduced with permission of Corbis/Art Wolfe. Backcover image of Vanuatu Vulcano reproduced with permission of Corbis/Larry Dale Gordon/zefa.

Contents

Landforms

The land is made of different shapes.
These shapes are called landforms.

volcano

A volcano is a landform.
A volcano is not living.

What Is a Volcano?

A volcano is a mountain with a hole on top.

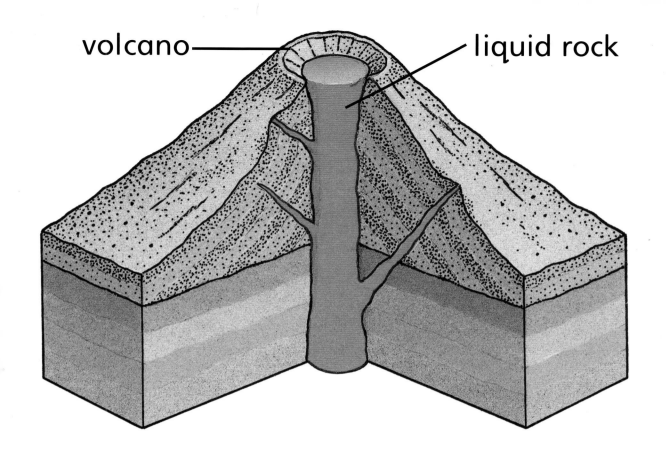

volcano —

liquid rock

The hole goes down to liquid rock.
Liquid rock is rock that runs like water.

Liquid rock can shoot out of a volcano.

The liquid rock is very hot.
The liquid rock is called lava.

Lava gets hard when it cools.

Lava can make a mountain.

Features of a Volcano

crater

A crater is a hole where the lava comes out.

cone

A cone is the shape of a volcano.

Where You Can Find Volcanoes

Some volcanoes are in warm places.

Some volcanoes are in cold places.

Some islands are underwater volcanoes.

Some volcanoes are close to each other.

What Lives Near a Volcano?

Plants grow near volcanoes.

People live near volcanoes.

Studying Volcanoes

Some people study volcanoes.

Volcanoes remind us how fast the earth can change.

Volcano Facts

Mauna Loa is a volcano. It is the largest volcano on Earth.

The planet Mars has a volcano. It is larger than volcanoes on Earth.